T0030073

To Olivia and Tenzin
—A.W.

I dedicate this book to my younger self, who
so desperately wanted to explore and see the
world one day. I hope I've made you proud.
—Q.M.

Katherine Tegen Books is an imprint of HarperCollins Publishers.

There Is a Flower at the Tip of My Nose Smelling Me
Text copyright © 2006 by Alice Walker
Illustrations copyright © 2022 by Queenbe Monyei
All rights reserved. Manufactured in Italy.
No part of this book may be used or reproduced in any manner whatsoever
without written permission except in the case of brief quotations embodied in
critical articles and reviews. For information address HarperCollins Children's Books,
a division of HarperCollins Publishers, 195 Broadway, New York, NY 10007.
www.harpercollinschildrens.com

Library of Congress Control Number: 2021933201
ISBN 978-0-06-308991-4

The artist used a combination of vector-based graphics
and photography to create the digital illustrations for this book.
Typography by Rachel Zegar
22 23 24 25 26   RTLO   10 9 8 7 6 5 4 3 2 1
❖
Originally published in 2006 by HarperCollins Publishers.

There Is a Flower at the Tip of My Nose Smelling Me

written by Alice Walker

illustrations by Queenbe Monyei

KATHERINE TEGEN BOOKS
An Imprint of HarperCollins Publishers

There is a flower
At the tip
Of my nose
Smelling
Me.

There is a sky
At the end
Of my eye
Seeing
Me.

There is a road
At the bottom
Of my
Foot
Walking me.

There is a dog
At the end
Of my leash
Holding
Me.

There is an ocean
At the top
Of my
Head
Swimming me.

There is a sunrise
At the edge
Of
My skin
Praising
Me.

There is water
At the tip
Of my tongue
Tasting me.

There is a song
Deep in
My body
Singing
Me.

There is a dance
That lives
In my bones
Dancing
Me.

There is a poem
In the cradle
Of my Soul
Rocking me.

writing me. There is a pen nestled in my hand writing me. There is a
There is a pen nestled in
There is a pen nestled in my hand

There is a pen
Nestled
In my hand
Writing
Me.

There is a story
At the end
Of my arms
Telling
Me!

There is a story at the end of my arms telling me! There is a story at the